CHECKERBOARD BIOGRAPHY LIBRARY

U.S. PRESIDENTS

The United States Presidents

JOHN ADAMS

ABDO Publishing Company

Heidi M.D. Elston

visit us at
www.abdopublishing.com

Published by ABDO Publishing Company, 8000 West 78th Street, Edina, Minnesota 55439.
Copyright © 2009 by Abdo Consulting Group, Inc. International copyrights reserved in all
countries. No part of this book may be reproduced in any form without written permission from the
publisher. The Checkerboard Library™ is a trademark and logo of ABDO Publishing Company.

Printed in the United States.

Cover Photo: Getty Images
Interior Photos: American Political History p. 24; AP Images p. 5; Corbis pp. 12, 17, 20, 22, 28, 29;
     Getty Images pp. 11, 13, 14–15, 16, 23; iStockphoto p. 32; National Archives p. 19; National
     Park Service pp. 9, 26; North Wind pp. 18, 21, 25, 27, 29

Editor: BreAnn Rumsch
Art Direction & Cover Design: Neil Klinepier
Interior Design: Jaime Martens

Library of Congress Cataloging-in-Publication Data

Elston, Heidi M.D., 1979-
  John Adams / Heidi M.D. Elston.
      p. cm. -- (The United States presidents)
  Includes index.
  ISBN 978-1-60453-439-9
  1. Adams, John, 1735-1826--Juvenile literature. 2. Presidents--United States--Biography--
Juvenile literature. I. Title.

  E322.E49 2009
  973.4'4092--dc22
  [B]

                                                            2008027037

CONTENTS

JOHN ADAMS

John Adams led the fight for a new, united country. He encouraged the North American colonies to break away from Great Britain. This led to the **American Revolution** and to the establishment of the United States of America.

Adams made several important contributions to American history. He helped write the Declaration of Independence and signed the document. He authored the Massachusetts **constitution**. Adams also nominated George Washington as the first commander of the Continental army. And, he helped put together the U.S. Navy.

Adams served his country during a time of great change. He was the first U.S. vice president and the second U.S. president. Many people argued with Adams about how to do his job. But, he did what he thought was best for Americans. Adams worked hard to bring peace to the United States.

TIMELINE

1735 - John Adams was born in Braintree, Massachusetts, on October 30.

1764 - On October 25, Adams married Abigail Smith.

1765 - The Stamp Act passed, requiring colonists to pay more money to Great Britain.

1770 - On March 5, five colonists were killed during the Boston Massacre.

1773 - About 60 colonists participated in the Boston Tea Party on December 16.

1774 - Adams attended the First Continental Congress in Philadelphia, Pennsylvania.

1775 - Adams attended the Second Continental Congress; George Washington was chosen to lead the newly formed Continental army; the American Revolution began.

1776 - On July 4, the Continental Congress approved the Declaration of Independence.

1780 - Adams authored the Massachusetts constitution.

1783 - Adams signed the Treaty of Paris, which officially ended the American Revolution.

1789 - Adams became the nation's first vice president.

1797 - On March 4, Adams became the second U.S. president.

1798 - Congress passed the Alien and Sedition Acts.

1800 - The U.S. Capitol moved from Philadelphia to Washington, D.C.

1818 - Abigail Adams died on October 28.

1825 - Adams's son John Quincy became the sixth U.S. president.

1826 - On July 4, John Adams died.

When John Adams was born, England's North American colonies used the Julian calendar. On that calendar, Adams's birthday was October 19. England and its colonies adopted the Gregorian calendar in 1752. Then, October 19 became October 30.

The home in which Adams was born is one of the oldest presidential birthplaces in the United States.

Adams was the first U.S. president to father a president.

Adams was the first president to live in the White House. When he moved in, only 6 of the 36 rooms were livable.

Abigail Adams was the first woman in U.S. history to be both the wife of one president and the mother of another president.

EARLY YEARS

John Adams was born in Braintree, Massachusetts, on October 30, 1735. At that time, Massachusetts was an English colony.

John's parents were John Adams and Susanna Boylston Adams. John adored his father. His father was a businessman, a farmer, and a church **deacon**. In many ways, young John was like his mother. Both John and Susanna liked to talk. And, they each had a hot temper.

John was the oldest of three boys. He spent much of his time outdoors, hiking and exploring. John liked to make and fly kites. He also swam, shot marbles, and played many sports.

Young John loved working on the family farm. He wanted to be a farmer when he grew up. But, his father wanted him to go to Harvard College to become a minister.

John learned to read at home. Then, he went to a **dame school** in a

FAST FACTS

BORN - October 30, 1735
WIFE - Abigail Smith
(1744–1818)
CHILDREN - 5
POLITICAL PARTY - Federalist
AGE AT INAUGURATION - 61
YEARS SERVED - 1797–1801
VICE PRESIDENT - Thomas Jefferson
DIED - July 4, 1826, age 90

8

John's birthplace in Braintree

neighbor's kitchen. There, he practiced reading and writing with other children.

Later, John attended the local school. But he didn't like his teacher, so he did poorly in his lessons. Soon, John's father allowed him to switch schools. In no time, John improved his studies.

John began preparing to go to Harvard College in Cambridge, Massachusetts. It was not easy to get accepted into Harvard. But John studied hard. When he was 15, he passed the school's entrance examinations.

COLLEGE AT HARVARD

In 1751, John left home to attend Harvard. Harvard had firm rules. Students had to get up very early in the morning. They studied most of the day. Then at night, they went to bed early.

John studied hard and earned good grades. His favorite subjects were mathematics and science. John also discovered he loved books. He began to read in earnest. From that time on, he was rarely without a book.

In 1755, John graduated from Harvard. Then, he moved to Worcester, Massachusetts, to begin teaching. In Worcester, John and his neighbors discussed politics. People talked a lot about wars in England and France. Both of these countries wanted land in the colonies.

John soon learned he did not like teaching. Instead, he decided to be a lawyer. He studied law for two years with Boston lawyer James Putnam. Then in 1758, John moved back to Braintree. There, he started his new job as a lawyer.

Harvard was founded in 1636. It is the oldest institution of higher learning in America.

JOHN AND ABIGAIL

Abigail was one of the most well-read women in America in the 1700s.

In 1759, John met a woman named Abigail Smith. The two became close friends. Abigail was very smart. In those days, most girls were not taught to read. But Abigail's parents had wanted their children to be educated. So, Abigail's mother had taught her to read.

Abigail loved books and politics. She also had a good sense of humor. Abigail and John enjoyed talking about the colonies and other countries. John had a strong temper that sometimes made him seem rough. But Abigail always smoothed things over.

On October 25, 1764, John and Abigail married. They had five children together. Sadly, Susannah died as a baby. The other children were Abigail, John Quincy, Charles, and Thomas.

The Adamses were very happy together. In Braintree, John farmed his land and built up his law business. He was the farmer he had always wanted to be. And, he had the education his father had always wanted for him.

John and Abigail lived in this home after they were married. John kept his law practice here. And, it was here that he later wrote the Massachusetts constitution.

FAIRNESS FOR ALL

In the 1760s, the colonies had to pay many taxes to Great Britain. In 1765, a new law called the Stamp Act demanded even more money. This angered colonists. Many colonists protested by refusing to use the stamps. And, **riots** broke out. Adams sided with the colonists. He said the tax was illegal. The act was **repealed** the next year.

In 1768, the Adams family moved to Boston, Massachusetts. There on March 5, 1770, a fight broke out between colonists and British soldiers. The soldiers killed five colonists. This is called the Boston Massacre.

The soldiers went on trial. Adams was afraid they would not get a fair trial. So he became their lawyer! Adams thought the colonists would be angry with him. But they respected him even more because he was fair. So, Adams was appointed to the Massachusetts House of Representatives.

The Boston Massacre helped lead to the American Revolution.

Trouble continued between the colonists and the British. In 1773, England passed a tax on tea shipped to the colonies. On December 16, colonists protested the tax. That night, American patriots climbed onto English ships in Boston Harbor. Then, they threw 342 chests filled with tea into the water. This incident is called the Boston Tea Party.

About 60 colonists participated in the Boston Tea Party. They were dressed as Mohawk Native Americans.

One year later, Adams attended a meeting in Philadelphia, Pennsylvania. Leaders from the colonies wanted to decide what to do about the English. The delegates made up the First Continental Congress. Like Adams, most of the delegates wanted the colonies to form their own country.

The Second Continental Congress met in 1775. While attending, Adams helped organize the Continental army. He also nominated George Washington as its commander in chief. The **American Revolution** had begun.

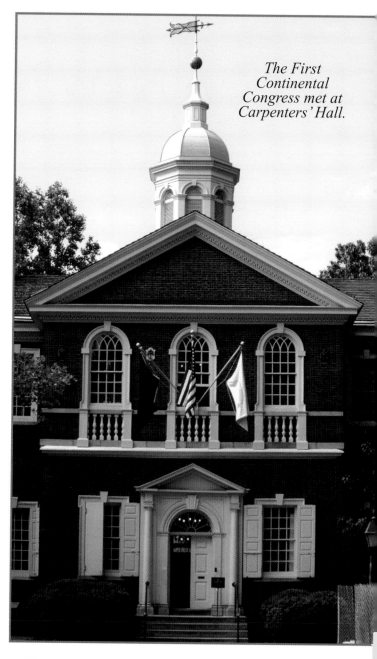

The First Continental Congress met at Carpenters' Hall.

A NEW NATION

By 1776, the Continental Congress agreed to break from England. Adams served on a special committee charged with an important task. This was to **draft** a statement declaring why the colonies should be free and independent.

The declaration drafting committee consisted of Thomas Jefferson, John Adams, Benjamin Franklin, Roger Sherman, and Robert R. Livingston.

Thomas Jefferson wrote most of the paper. When it was finished, Adams defended the paper before Congress. On July 4, 1776, the Continental Congress approved the Declaration of Independence. The United States of America was born. And, the colonies were declared independent states.

Declaration of Independence

Adams remained a leader in the Continental Congress. He was made head of the Board of War and Ordnance. This committee was responsible for equipping the army. It was at this time that Adams created the American navy.

From 1778 to 1779, Adams spent time in France. He wanted the French to help the Americans in the war.

Adams then returned to the United States. In Massachusetts, he joined the convention to write the state's **constitution**. Adams finished writing the document in 1780. It stated the laws and rules for Massachusetts. Many states modeled their constitutions after Adams's document.

Congress then sent Adams to France to **negotiate** an end to the war. He took his sons John Quincy and Charles with him. Adams missed his wife and his other children terribly. Mr. and Mrs. Adams exchanged many letters.

Meanwhile, the **American Revolution** was still being fought. The United States gained an important victory in late 1781. On October 19, the British surrendered at Yorktown, Virginia. It took Adams two more years to get England to sign a peace treaty. The Treaty of Paris was signed on September 3, 1783. Adams was one of the signers. The treaty officially ended the American Revolution.

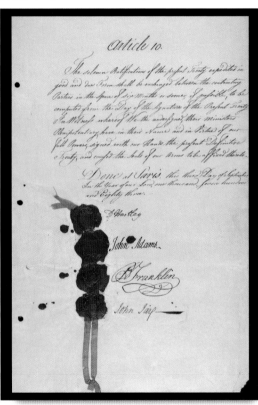

Treaty of Paris

In 1785, the rest of the Adams family traveled to France. Then, the family moved to England. There, Adams worked to keep the peace between America and England.

While Adams was away, most states approved the U.S. **Constitution**. This document named a new U.S. Congress as head of the federal government.

In 1788, the Adams family returned home. The next year, Congress voted for the first president of the United States. George Washington received the most votes, so he became president. Adams had the second-highest number of votes. So, he became vice president.

Washington took office on April 30, 1789, in New York City, New York.

PRESIDENT ADAMS

When Adams took office, times were hard. People argued about wars in Europe and about land in the western United States. Adams remained vice president under Washington in the 1792 election.

In the 1796 election, Adams ran as a **Federalist** against **Democratic-Republican** Thomas Jefferson. Adams received three more votes than Jefferson did. So, Adams became the second U.S. president. Jefferson became his vice president. Adams took office on March 4, 1797.

Vice President Jefferson

Soon, Adams had trouble with Jefferson and Congress. There was a revolution in France. Many French people were fighting their government.

Vice President Jefferson wanted to help the French people with their war. But, President Adams wanted to make peace with the French government. This decision angered Jefferson and many members of Congress. It would cost Adams the next election.

PRESIDENT ADAMS'S CABINET

MARCH 4, 1797–
MARCH 4, 1801

- **STATE** – Timothy Pickering
  John Marshall (from June 6, 1800)
- **TREASURY** – Oliver Wolcott Jr.
  Samuel Dexter (from January 1, 1801)
- **WAR** – James McHenry
  Samuel Dexter (from June 12, 1800)
- **NAVY** – Benjamin Stoddert (from June 18, 1798)
- **ATTORNEY GENERAL** – Charles Lee

In 1798, the **Federalist**-controlled Congress passed the Alien and Sedition Acts. The Alien Acts allowed the president to **deport** foreigners. The Sedition Act made it a crime to criticize the U.S. government and its leaders.

President Adams signed the Alien and Sedition Acts under pressure from his party. The acts quickly met with much disapproval. Vice President Jefferson said they were **unconstitutional**. Adams soon realized they were a mistake.

In 1800, the U.S. Capitol moved from Philadelphia to Washington, D.C. Adams was the first president to live in

The new Capitol in 1800

SUPREME COURT APPOINTMENTS

BUSHROD WASHINGTON - 1799
ALFRED MOORE - 1800
JOHN MARSHALL - 1801

the presidential mansion, now called the White House. The house wasn't even finished when he moved in! There were weeds, tree stumps, and stones all around it. But the First Lady held dinners and parties there anyway.

President Adams and Vice President Jefferson faced off in the 1800 presidential election. This time, Jefferson won the most votes. Before his term ended in 1801, Adams named John Marshall as **chief justice** of the **Supreme Court**.

Chief Justice John Marshall was one of Adams's most important court appointments. Marshall served on the U.S. Supreme Court for 34 years.

RETURN TO QUINCY

Adams was hurt and sad when he lost the election. He left Washington, D.C., without saying good-bye to Jefferson. Mr. and Mrs. Adams went home to Braintree, now called Quincy. The people in their hometown were still their good friends. The Adamses hosted parties for friends and neighbors. Adams also wrote many letters and articles.

The Adams family home in Quincy is called the Old House. It was built in 1731.

Over the years, Mr. and Mrs. Adams had spent much time apart. They relied heavily on letter writing to keep in touch. These letters provide historians with information about the couple's loving relationship.

In 1812, Adams decided to write Jefferson. He wanted to renew their friendship. The attempt worked! At last they were friends again. Over the next many years, Adams and Jefferson exchanged 160 letters.

On October 28, 1818, Abigail Adams died. Adams was very sad. He wrote many letters to Jefferson about how much he missed her.

In 1825, Adams's son John Quincy became the sixth U.S. president. This made Adams proud. But, he did not get to see his son act as president for long.

John Quincy Adams served as president from 1825 to 1829.

John and Abigail Adams are buried in Quincy at the United First Parish Church.

John Adams died on July 4, 1826. This was the fiftieth anniversary of the approval of the Declaration of Independence. The last thing he said was, "Thomas Jefferson survives." Adams didn't know it, but Jefferson had died just a few hours earlier.

Adams is remembered for his great contributions to U.S. history. He supported freedom for the colonies. He helped **draft** the Declaration of Independence. In addition, Adams wrote the Massachusetts **constitution**. He also led the formation of an American army and navy. Above all, John Adams promoted peace for his new country.

OFFICE OF THE PRESIDENT

BRANCHES OF GOVERNMENT

The U.S. government is divided into three branches. They are the executive, legislative, and judicial branches. This division is called a separation of powers. Each branch has some power over the others. This is called a system of checks and balances.

EXECUTIVE BRANCH

The executive branch enforces laws. It is made up of the president, the vice president, and the president's cabinet. The president represents the United States around the world. He or she oversees relations with other countries and signs treaties. The president signs bills into law and appoints officials and federal judges. He or she also leads the military and manages government workers.

LEGISLATIVE BRANCH

The legislative branch makes laws, maintains the military, and regulates trade. It also has the power to declare war. This branch consists of the Senate and the House of Representatives. Together, these two houses make up Congress. Each state has two senators. A state's population determines the number of representatives it has.

JUDICIAL BRANCH

The judicial branch interprets laws. It consists of district courts, courts of appeals, and the Supreme Court. District courts try cases. If a person disagrees with a trial's outcome, he or she may appeal. If the courts of appeals support the ruling, a person may appeal to the Supreme Court. The Supreme Court also makes sure that laws follow the U.S. Constitution.

QUALIFICATIONS FOR OFFICE

To be president, a person must meet three requirements. A candidate must be at least 35 years old and a natural-born U.S. citizen. He or she must also have lived in the United States for at least 14 years.

ELECTORAL COLLEGE

The U.S. presidential election is an indirect election. Voters from each state choose electors to represent them in the Electoral College. The number of electors from each state is based on population. Each elector has one electoral vote. Electors are pledged to cast their vote for the candidate who receives the highest number of popular votes in their state. A candidate must receive the majority of Electoral College votes to win.

TERM OF OFFICE

Each president may be elected to two four-year terms. Sometimes, a president may only be elected once. This happens if he or she served more than two years of the previous president's term.

The presidential election is held on the Tuesday after the first Monday in November. The president is sworn in on January 20 of the following year. At that time, he or she takes the oath of office:

I do solemnly swear (or affirm) that I will faithfully execute the office of President of the United States, and will to the best of my ability, preserve, protect and defend the Constitution of the United States.

LINE OF SUCCESSION

The Presidential Succession Act of 1947 defines who becomes president if the president cannot serve. The vice president is first in the line of succession. Next are the Speaker of the House and the President Pro Tempore of the Senate. If none of these individuals is able to serve, the office falls to the president's cabinet members. They would take office in the order in which each department was created:

Secretary of State
Secretary of the Treasury
Secretary of Defense
Attorney General
Secretary of the Interior
Secretary of Agriculture
Secretary of Commerce
Secretary of Labor
Secretary of Health and Human Services
Secretary of Housing and Urban Development
Secretary of Transportation
Secretary of Energy
Secretary of Education
Secretary of Veterans Affairs
Secretary of Homeland Security

BENEFITS

• While in office, the president receives a salary of $400,000 each year. He or she lives in the White House and has 24-hour Secret Service protection.

• The president may travel on a Boeing 747 jet called Air Force One. The airplane can accommodate 70 passengers. It has kitchens, a dining room, sleeping areas, and a conference room. It also has fully equipped offices with the latest communications systems. Air Force One can fly halfway around the world before needing to refuel. It can even refuel in flight!

• If the president wishes to travel by car, he or she uses Cadillac One. Cadillac One is a Cadillac Deville. It has been modified with heavy armor and communications systems. The president takes Cadillac One along when visiting other countries if secure transportation will be needed.

• The president also travels on a helicopter called Marine One. Like the presidential car, Marine One accompanies the president when traveling abroad if necessary.

• Sometimes, the president needs to get away and relax with family and friends. Camp David is the official presidential retreat. It is located in the cool, wooded mountains in Maryland. The U.S. Navy maintains the retreat, and the U.S. Marine Corps keeps it secure. The camp offers swimming, tennis, golf, and hiking.

• When the president leaves office, he or she receives Secret Service protection for ten more years. He or she also receives a yearly pension of $191,300 and funding for office space, supplies, and staff.

PRESIDENTS AND THEIR TERMS

PRESIDENT	PARTY	TOOK OFFICE	LEFT OFFICE	TERMS SERVED	VICE PRESIDENT
George Washington	None	April 30, 1789	March 4, 1797	Two	John Adams
John Adams	Federalist	March 4, 1797	March 4, 1801	One	Thomas Jefferson
Thomas Jefferson	Democratic-Republican	March 4, 1801	March 4, 1809	Two	Aaron Burr, George Clinton
James Madison	Democratic-Republican	March 4, 1809	March 4, 1817	Two	George Clinton, Elbridge Gerry
James Monroe	Democratic-Republican	March 4, 1817	March 4, 1825	Two	Daniel D. Tompkins
John Quincy Adams	Democratic-Republican	March 4, 1825	March 4, 1829	One	John C. Calhoun
Andrew Jackson	Democrat	March 4, 1829	March 4, 1837	Two	John C. Calhoun, Martin Van Buren
Martin Van Buren	Democrat	March 4, 1837	March 4, 1841	One	Richard M. Johnson
William H. Harrison	Whig	March 4, 1841	April 4, 1841	Died During First Term	John Tyler
John Tyler	Whig	April 6, 1841	March 4, 1845	Completed Harrison's Term	Office Vacant
James K. Polk	Democrat	March 4, 1845	March 4, 1849	One	George M. Dallas
Zachary Taylor	Whig	March 5, 1849	July 9, 1850	Died During First Term	Millard Fillmore

PRESIDENT	PARTY	TOOK OFFICE	LEFT OFFICE	TERMS SERVED	VICE PRESIDENT
Millard Fillmore	Whig	July 10, 1850	March 4, 1853	Completed Taylor's Term	Office Vacant
Franklin Pierce	Democrat	March 4, 1853	March 4, 1857	One	William R.D. King
James Buchanan	Democrat	March 4, 1857	March 4, 1861	One	John C. Breckinridge
Abraham Lincoln	Republican	March 4, 1861	April 15, 1865	Served One Term, Died During Second Term	Hannibal Hamlin, Andrew Johnson
Andrew Johnson	Democrat	April 15, 1865	March 4, 1869	Completed Lincoln's Second Term	Office Vacant
Ulysses S. Grant	Republican	March 4, 1869	March 4, 1877	Two	Schuyler Colfax, Henry Wilson
Rutherford B. Hayes	Republican	March 3, 1877	March 4, 1881	One	William A. Wheeler
James A. Garfield	Republican	March 4, 1881	September 19, 1881	Died During First Term	Chester Arthur
Chester Arthur	Republican	September 20, 1881	March 4, 1885	Completed Garfield's Term	Office Vacant
Grover Cleveland	Democrat	March 4, 1885	March 4, 1889	One	Thomas A. Hendricks
Benjamin Harrison	Republican	March 4, 1889	March 4, 1893	One	Levi P. Morton
Grover Cleveland	Democrat	March 4, 1893	March 4, 1897	One	Adlai E. Stevenson
William McKinley	Republican	March 4, 1897	September 14, 1901	Served One Term, Died During Second Term	Garret A. Hobart, Theodore Roosevelt

PRESIDENT	PARTY	TOOK OFFICE	LEFT OFFICE	TERMS SERVED	VICE PRESIDENT
Theodore Roosevelt	Republican	September 14, 1901	March 4, 1909	Completed McKinley's Second Term, Served One Term	Office Vacant, Charles Fairbanks
William Taft	Republican	March 4, 1909	March 4, 1913	One	James S. Sherman
Woodrow Wilson	Democrat	March 4, 1913	March 4, 1921	Two	Thomas R. Marshall
Warren G. Harding	Republican	March 4, 1921	August 2, 1923	Died During First Term	Calvin Coolidge
Calvin Coolidge	Republican	August 3, 1923	March 4, 1929	Completed Harding's Term, Served One Term	Office Vacant, Charles Dawes
Herbert Hoover	Republican	March 4, 1929	March 4, 1933	One	Charles Curtis
Franklin D. Roosevelt	Democrat	March 4, 1933	April 12, 1945	Served Three Terms, Died During Fourth Term	John Nance Garner, Henry A. Wallace, Harry S. Truman
Harry S. Truman	Democrat	April 12, 1945	January 20, 1953	Completed Roosevelt's Fourth Term, Served One Term	Office Vacant, Alben Barkley
Dwight D. Eisenhower	Republican	January 20, 1953	January 20, 1961	Two	Richard Nixon
John F. Kennedy	Democrat	January 20, 1961	November 22, 1963	Died During First Term	Lyndon B. Johnson
Lyndon B. Johnson	Democrat	November 22, 1963	January 20, 1969	Completed Kennedy's Term, Served One Term	Office Vacant, Hubert H. Humphrey
Richard Nixon	Republican	January 20, 1969	August 9, 1974	Completed First Term, Resigned During Second Term	Spiro T. Agnew, Gerald Ford

PRESIDENT	PARTY	TOOK OFFICE	LEFT OFFICE	TERMS SERVED	VICE PRESIDENT
Gerald Ford	Republican	August 9, 1974	January 20, 1977	Completed Nixon's Second Term	Nelson A. Rockefeller
Jimmy Carter	Democrat	January 20, 1977	January 20, 1981	One	Walter Mondale
Ronald Reagan	Republican	January 20, 1981	January 20, 1989	Two	George H.W. Bush
George H.W. Bush	Republican	January 20, 1989	January 20, 1993	One	Dan Quayle
Bill Clinton	Democrat	January 20, 1993	January 20, 2001	Two	Al Gore
George W. Bush	Republican	January 20, 2001	January 20, 2009	Two	Dick Cheney
Barack Obama	Democrat	January 20, 2009			Joe Biden

"A government of laws and not of men." *John Adams*

WRITE TO THE PRESIDENT

You may write to the president at:

**The White House
1600 Pennsylvania Avenue NW
Washington, DC 20500**

You may e-mail the president at:
comments@whitehouse.gov

GLOSSARY

American Revolution - from 1775 to 1783. A war for independence between Great Britain and its North American colonies. The colonists won and created the United States of America.

chief justice - the head judge of the U.S. Supreme Court.

constitution - the laws that govern a country or a state. The U.S. Constitution is the laws that govern the United States.

dame school - a school in which basic skills such as reading and writing were taught by a woman in her own home.

deacon - a church officer who helps the minister in church duties not connected with the preaching.

Democratic-Republican - a member of the Democratic-Republican political party. During the early 1800s, Democratic-Republicans believed in weak national government and strong state government.

deport - to force someone who is not a citizen to leave the country.

draft - to compose or prepare.

Federalist - a member of the Federalist political party. During the early 1800s, Federalists believed in a strong national government.

negotiate (nih-GOH-shee-ayt) - to work out an agreement about the terms of a contract.

repeal - to formally withdraw or cancel.

riot - a sometimes violent disturbance caused by a large group of people.

Supreme Court - the highest, most powerful court in the United States.

unconstitutional - something that goes against the laws of a constitution.

WEB SITES

To learn more about John Adams, visit ABDO Publishing Company on the World Wide Web at **www.abdopublishing.com**. Web sites about John Adams are featured on our Book Links page. These links are routinely monitored and updated to provide the most current information available.

INDEX